HABITAT SURVIVAL

DESERTS

Melanie Waldron

www.raintreepublishers.co.uk
Visit our website to find out more information about Raintree books.

To order:
☎ Phone 0845 6044371
▤ Fax +44 (0) 1865 312263
▣ Email myorders@raintreepublishers.co.uk

Customers from outside the UK please telephone +44 1865 312262

Raintree is an imprint of Capstone Global Library Limited, a company incorporated in England and Wales having its registered office at 7 Pilgrim Street, London, EC4V 6LB – Registered company number: 6695582

Text © Capstone Global Library Limited 2013
First published in hardback in 2013
The moral rights of the proprietor have been asserted.

Edited by Nancy Dickmann, Kristen Kowalkowski, and Claire Throp
Designed by Philippa Jenkins
Original illustrations © Capstone Global Library Ltd 2013
Illustrations by Oxford Designers & Illustrators, and Words and Publications
Picture research by Tracy Cummins
Originated by Capstone Global Library Ltd
Printed and bound in China by CTPS

ISBN 978 1 406 23990 4 (hardback)
16 15 14 13 12
10 9 8 7 6 5 4 3 2 1

British Library Cataloguing in Publication Data
Waldron, Melanie.
Deserts. -- (Habitat survival)
577.5'4-dc23
A full catalogue record for this book is available from the British Library.

Acknowledgements
We would like to thank the following for permission to reproduce photographs: Corbis pp. 8 (© Randi Hirschmann/Science Faction), 27 (© George H.H. Huey); FLPA p. 22 (ImageBroker/Imagebroker); Getty Images pp. 15 (Wayne Lynch), 17 (Marty Cordano), 20 (Ernesto Benavides/AFP), 23 (Daniel Garcia/AFP); National Geographic Stock p. 10 (Joel Sartore); Nature Picture Library pp. 12 (Ashish & Shanthi Chandola), 14 (Solvin Zankl); Nevada Native Plant Society p. 7 (USDA-NRCS PLANTS Database); Shutterstock pp. 5 (© Galyna Andrushko), 6 (© Synchronista), 9 (© Pascal Rateau), 11 (© EcoPrint), 13 (© PhotoSky 4t com), 18 (© Jens Peermann), 19 (© Fremme), 21 (© Hector Conesa); Still Pictures p. 25 (Mark Edwards); Superstock p. 29 (The Travel Library).

Cover photograph of a male gilded flicker in a saguaro cactus reproduced with permission of Corbis/© Visuals Unlimited.

Every effort has been made to contact copyright holders of any material reproduced in this book. Any omissions will be rectified in subsequent printings if notice is given to the publisher.

Disclaimer
All the internet addresses (URLs) given in this book were valid at the time of going to press. However, due to the dynamic nature of the internet, some addresses may have changed, or sites may have changed or ceased to exist since publication. While the author and publisher regret any inconvenience this may cause readers, no responsibility for any such changes can be accepted by either the author or the publisher.

Contents

Some words are shown in bold, **like this**. You can find out what they mean by looking in the glossary.

Dry, dry, dry!

Deserts are the world's driest areas. They receive very little rain or snow each year. Deserts are usually baking hot, like the Sahara Desert in Africa. However, they can also be cold, like the Gobi Desert in Asia. Cold deserts are usually sandy, rocky, and icy. Snow may sometimes fall. Deserts are often very windy. Rainfall usually comes in big storms, only a few times a year.

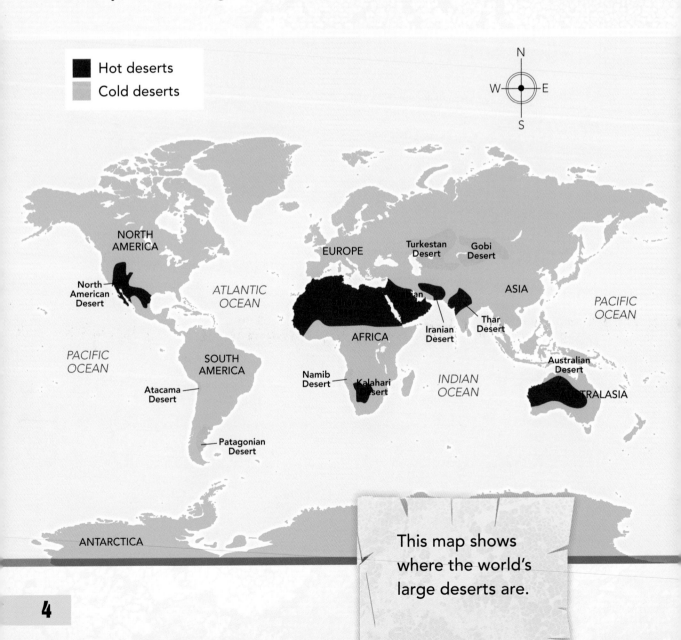

■ Hot deserts
■ Cold deserts

N
W—●—E
S

NORTH AMERICA

North American Desert

ATLANTIC OCEAN

EUROPE

Turkestan Desert

Gobi Desert

ASIA

PACIFIC OCEAN

PACIFIC OCEAN

SOUTH AMERICA

Atacama Desert

Namib Desert

Kalahari Desert

AFRICA

Iranian Desert

Thar Desert

INDIAN OCEAN

Australian Desert

AUSTRALASIA

Patagonian Desert

ANTARCTICA

This map shows where the world's large deserts are.

It is amazing to think that, even in deserts, life can be found.

Hot deserts

Some hot deserts have huge sand **dunes**. Others are rocky, or covered in dried mud. The air is very dry and there are hardly any clouds. Daytime temperatures can be high – over 50 degrees Celsius (122 degrees Fahrenheit)! At night, it can get very cold. This is because there are no clouds to hold the heat in.

All living things – plants and animals – need water. With so little water available in deserts, how do living things survive? Desert **habitats** are places where some **unique** plants and animals can be found.

Coldest desert

The frozen Antarctic is also a desert! Some places there hardly get any rain or snow at all.

Desert plants

Most plants need a regular supply of water. In deserts, some areas go for years with no rainfall. Desert plants have **adapted** to cope with this. They must also cope with very hot days and very cold nights.

The cactus is the most famous desert plant. There are lots of different kinds of cacti. They have thick, swollen stems that can store lots of water. Some have strong, sharp spikes to stop animals from eating them.

The saguaro cactus has very fine, hairy spines. These create a layer of still air around the cactus, protecting it from hot, drying winds.

Finding water

The welwitschia plant grows in the Namib Desert in Africa. Its leaves **absorb** tiny droplets of water from the fog that drifts across the desert. Some desert plants have extremely long roots that grow deep into the ground to find water. Others have roots that spread out over a huge area, to soak up any water they can find.

Desert anemone flowers grow in very dry, rocky places.

Underground stores

Some plants have thick underground **tubers**. These are swollen parts of the roots. They can store food and water for the plant.

Blooming and beautiful

Deserts can be transformed after rainfall. Seeds in the ground lie in wait for a heavy rainstorm. Then, overnight, the seeds grow into little plants. In a few days, the desert floor can be a beautiful carpet of flowers. A few weeks later, when the ground dries up again, the plants die back. They leave behind more seeds, which wait for the next rainstorm to help them grow.

Deserts can spring to life after a rainstorm.

Exploding plants

When rain hits some desert plants, it can cause the seed pods to pop open. Some plants shoot their seeds high into the air, scattering them over the ground.

An oasis can create a small patch of green in a desert.

Oases

Many weary desert travellers dream of finding an **oasis** – a small area in a desert where water can be found. The water usually comes from under ground, where it is trapped between layers of rock. Lots of plants, such as palm trees, can grow well around oases.

Angled leaves

Desert holly grows in some US deserts. It turns its leaves throughout the day, so that only the leaf edges face the Sun. This stops the leaves from losing too much water.

Desert animals – keeping cool

Desert animals have to survive hot days and freezing nights. Fennec foxes have a coat of fur to keep them warm at night. However, the fur also helps to keep them cool during the day. This is because it is a light colour, and this **reflects** the Sun's heat.

Jackrabbits lose heat through their large ears. There are large **veins** running through the ears. As the jackrabbits move around, the air flowing over their ears helps to cool them down.

Jackrabbits use their ears to help cool themselves down.

Sunshade or blanket?

Desert squirrels flip their bushy tails over their backs during the day. This gives them shade from the Sun. At night, the squirrel uses its tail to keep warm!

Cooling down, warming up

Many animals cool down by panting or sweating. Tortoises dribble **saliva** over their necks to keep cool. Kangaroos scrape away the hot sand on the ground. They lie down in the cooler sand underneath. To warm up after a cold night, roadrunner birds lift the feathers on their necks. Under these feathers is a special area of skin which **absorbs** the Sun's heat.

Stay out of the Sun!

Small desert animals can keep cool simply by staying out of the Sun. Some burrow into the ground or hide under rocks and stones. Many are nocturnal. This means that they sleep during the hot day, and come out in the cooler night to hunt and feed.

Woodpeckers use their beaks to poke holes in damaged parts of saguaro cactus plants. They can climb inside the cactus and nest there, out of the Sun.

Gerbils stay in their underground burrows during hot desert days. They come out at night when it is much cooler.

Legless lizards

The legless skink looks like a snake, but is actually a lizard without legs! It moves through the cooler layers of sand below the surface. Having no legs allows it to move more easily through the sand. The skink's eyes have a protective cover to keep the sand out.

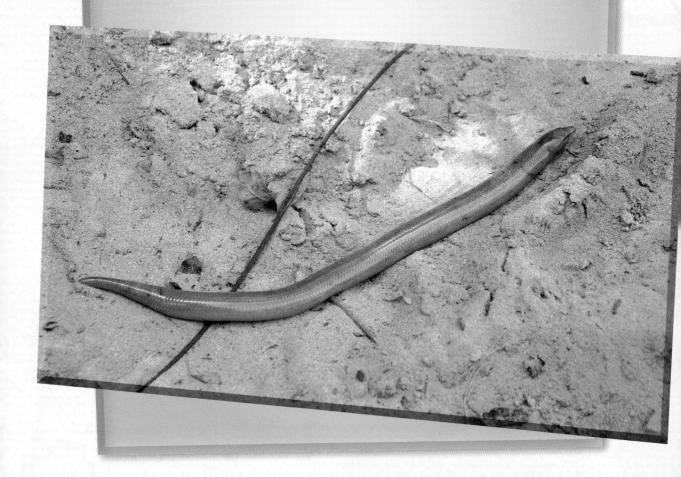

Underground toads

Spadefoot toads bury themselves in the ground and can stay there for up to 10 months! After heavy rainfall, they wriggle up to the surface. There they **breed** and lay their eggs. They must burrow down again before the ground dries up a few days later.

Finding water

Many small desert animals get all the water they need from their food. However, the fog-basking beetle in the Namib Desert has a clever way of getting water. It stands on top of sand **dunes** with its back end raised up. As fog drifts over the dunes, little droplets of water form on its back. These run down into its mouth.

Feeding by feather

Male sandgrouse birds soak their feathers in any pools of water they find. They fly back to their nests, and their chicks suck the water from the feathers.

The fog-basking beetle raises its back to tip water droplets into its mouth.

Desert honey ants have stomachs that can swell up. They store liquid food called nectar in these stomachs.

Clever gerbils

Gerbils store dry seeds in their burrows. While the gerbils sleep, the seeds **absorb** the moisture from their breath. When the gerbils wake up, they eat the seeds and get this precious moisture back!

Big drinkers

Larger animals, such as camels and oryx, must travel to find water to drink. Camels can drink a huge amount of water in one go – up to 140 litres (37 gallons)! This will last them about a week, and then they must drink again.

Desert food webs

All living things need **energy** to survive. Plants get their energy from the Sun's light. They use this to make food for themselves. Some animals eat plants to get their energy. Some animals eat other animals, and some eat both plants and animals. The energy in a **food chain** passes from plant to animal to animal, and so on. A food web is made of lots of connecting food chains.

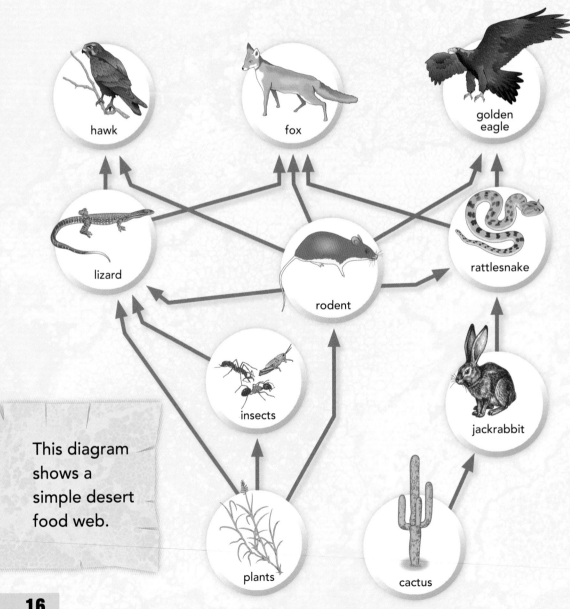

This diagram shows a simple desert food web.

Gila monsters are lizards which live in deserts in the United States. They eat small mammals, insects, bird eggs, and baby birds.

Plant eaters

In desert **habitats**, there is plenty of sunlight for plants to make food. However, plants struggle to grow because there is so little water. Animals that eat plants and insects, such as jerboas, are called omnivores.

Animals that eat other animals are called carnivores. For example, geckos eat beetles and other insects, and fennec foxes eat gerbils.

Predators and prey

Animals that hunt and eat other animals are called predators. The animals they hunt are called prey. Some predators have very clever ways of hunting and catching their food. However, some prey have very clever ways of avoiding being caught!

The Moloch lizard of Australia sits quietly beside lines of marching ants. With a flick of its long tongue, it catches ants one by one and eats them. Some desert spiders build webbed trapdoors across their burrows. These catch any insects that wander too close.

Tarantula spiders use their fangs to inject **venom** into their prey. Then they suck up the prey's insides.

Chuckwalla lizards wedge themselves into cracks in the rock to avoid predators. They puff up their bodies so that predators cannot pull them out.

Hiding to keep safe

Many animals use **camouflage** to hide from predators. A horned lizard has grey-brown skin covered in little bumps and prickles. This makes it blend in on the sandy, rocky ground, as it hides from predators such as hawks.

Jump!

Kangaroo rats hop around on their back legs, a bit like kangaroos! They use these strong legs to leap out of the reach of predators such as foxes. When they land, they can change direction very quickly, confusing their hunters.

Desert dwellers

People across the world live in deserts. They have learned how to survive in this tough environment. Finding water is the key to their survival. Women from the Tubu tribe in the Sahara Desert have an amazing talent for remembering where their precious water wells are.

Fog nets

New technology is helping to bring water to desert people around the world. Huge nets, similar to volleyball nets, can catch the tiny water droplets in fog. This water runs down the nets into collection barrels, ready for people to use.

People in Mali, in North Africa, use mud and clay to build homes in the Sahara Desert.

Moving around

Many desert people are **nomads**. This means that they do not live in one place. They travel around from place to place, finding new areas to **graze** their animals and collect water. Nomads in the Gobi Desert can put up their beautiful tents, called yurts, in around one hour. These circular homes keep people warm in the freezing desert nights.

Many people in the Sahara Desert and the Gobi Desert rely on camels to travel huge distances. They often travel to **oases**, where towns and villages can be found. Here, people meet to buy and sell goods.

Harmful activities

Desert **habitats** across the world are being harmed by human activities. **Mining** for **minerals** such as salt, and for precious gemstones has harmed some areas. Drilling for oil is also damaging deserts across the world.

This is part of an opal mine in Coober Pedy, Australia. Opals are gemstones.

Desert racing

The Dakar is a motor vehicle race. It once went from Paris in France to Dakar in Senegal, Africa, crossing parts of the Sahara. It is now held in Argentina and Chile, crossing areas of desert. Some people are worried about the damage that the cars, motorbikes, and lorries do to the desert habitats.

Tourism

Tourism in desert areas is a growing problem, as more people want to visit these special places. Tourists use water and some leave behind waste and litter. Hunting animals is also damaging desert habitats. The oryx in the Arabian Desert has long been hunted, and is now **endangered**.

Expanding deserts

Human activity is affecting deserts by making them larger.
This happens when land around the edges of deserts is not
properly looked after, and it becomes part of the desert. This
is called **desertification**.

Farming on the edges of deserts is a big cause of desertification.
Animals eat too many plants and trample the soil, and the wind
can blow the soil away. This also happens when trees are cut
down, because the roots no longer hold the soil. Growing crops
can weaken the soil, too.

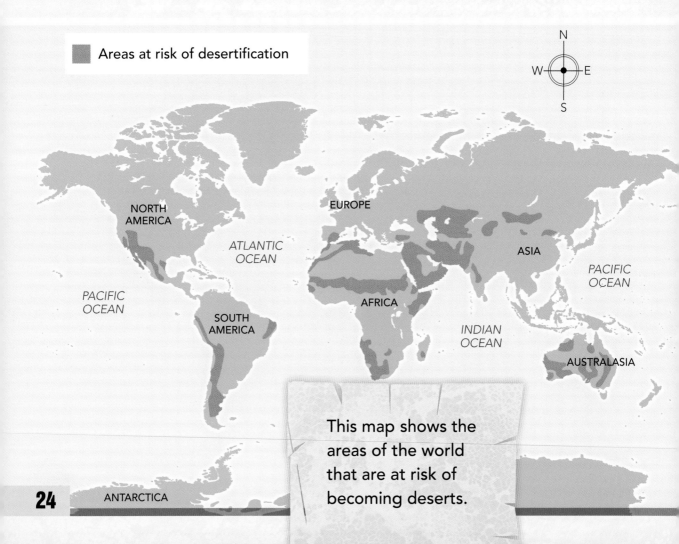

Areas at risk of desertification

NORTH
AMERICA

EUROPE

ATLANTIC
OCEAN

ASIA

PACIFIC
OCEAN

PACIFIC
OCEAN

AFRICA

SOUTH
AMERICA

INDIAN
OCEAN

AUSTRALASIA

ANTARCTICA

This map shows the
areas of the world
that are at risk of
becoming deserts.

These dead trees are in the Sahel, on the edge of the Sahara Desert. The land here is slowly turning into desert.

Getting hotter

Global warming is also causing desertification. Global warming is caused by human activity that releases harmful gases into the air. Activity in one part of the world can therefore affect the whole planet.

The Great Green Wall

The Great Green Wall is a plan to stop desertification on the south edge of the Sahara Desert. Eleven African countries plan to plant a huge wall of trees and bushes. It will be 15 kilometres (9.3 miles) wide and about 8,000 kilometres (4,970 miles) long. People hope that this will stop the desert spreading, and that it will provide people with food and other goods.

The struggle to survive

The world's population is growing. This means that more food needs to be grown. Some areas in the desert are being used to grow food. Water can be piped in from other areas to **irrigate** the land, so people can grow crops on it. This changes the desert **habitat**, sometimes for the better, but sometimes not.

Animals in danger

Some desert animals are struggling to survive because human activities are affecting deserts. The lappet-faced vulture often eats animals such as jackals. Some farmers in the desert poison jackals to stop them eating their farm animals. This means the vultures also die from poisoning. They are now **vulnerable**.

Some animals are surviving because people are working to protect them. People are no longer allowed to hunt the Peruvian desert fox, for example. The Eureka Valley evening primrose grows in the desert in California, USA. It was being destroyed by off-road vehicles until they were banned from certain areas.

Banning vehicles

The fringe-toed lizard in Colorado, USA, was threatened because of building development and vehicles. Vehicles have now been banned from some of its habitat areas.

The evening primrose grows in California, USA.

Tomorrow's desert habitats

The plants and animals living in deserts have **adapted** to cope with the high temperatures and the lack of water. However, desert **habitats** are easily damaged, and are at risk from different types of human activity. Deserts are also growing faster than they would naturally, as **desertification** takes place on desert edges. This is destroying other important habitats.

How can you help?

You can do lots of things to help desert habitats survive and to help slow down desertification:

- Find out more about deserts – read books and research websites.

- Join a conservation group that protects desert species.

- Adopt an animal that lives in the desert.

- Be **energy** wise to help reduce **global warming**.

- Use water wisely – it is a precious **resource**.

- Tell your friends and family so they can help, too.

These young children in the Gobi Desert are playing next to their school.

Learning from desert people

Humans have lived in deserts for thousands of years. Desert people know how to live alongside the plants and animals they share the land with. We should use their knowledge, and ours, to make sure we protect desert habitats.

Glossary

absorb take in or soak up

adapt change in order to survive in a particular place

breed mate and produce young

camouflage colour or pattern used by an animal or insect to blend into the background

desertification land turning into desert

dune large mound of sand built up by the wind

endangered threatened with dying out

energy power needed to grow, move, and live

food chain series of living things that provide food for each other

global warming increase in Earth's temperature, caused by chemicals in the air that trap the Sun's heat

graze eat grass and other green plants

habitat place where a plant or animal lives

irrigate supply water to land

mineral substance formed in the ground that is often valuable to people

mining digging deep into the ground to search for substances such as salt, gemstones, and oil

nomad person who has no fixed home and moves from place to place to find food, water, and grazing land for his or her animals

oasis (plural: **oases**) area in a desert with water, where plants can grow

reflect throw back from a surface

resource something of value that can be used

saliva liquid made in the mouth that helps with chewing food

tuber underground part of plant that is short, thick, and round

unique unlike anything else

vein thin tube that carries blood around the body

venom poison made by some animals

vulnerable likely to become endangered unless the situation improves

Find out more

Books

Desert Food Chains (Protecting Food Chains), Buffy Silverman (Raintree, 2011)

Deserts (Kingfisher Young Knowledge), Nicola Davies (Kingfisher Books, 2007)

Deserts (Extreme Habitats), Jim Page (TickTock, 2007)

Deserts Around the World (Geography Now), Jen Green (Wayland, 2008)

Websites

animals.nationalgeographic.com/animals
You can find out about all kinds of desert animals on National Geographic's website. Just search for the animal you want to find out about.

www.alicespringsdesertpark.com.au/kids/desert/index. shtml
Find out more about Australian deserts on this website.

www.bbc.co.uk/nature/habitats/Deserts_and_xeric_ shrublands
Watch film clips about some of the amazing plants and animals found in deserts.

www.desertmuseum.org/kids/online_fun.php
You can learn all about the Sonoran Desert in the United States on this website. There are lots of photos, questions and answers, and fact sheets.

panda.org/about_our_earth/ecoregions/about/habitat_ types/habitats/deserts
The WWF (World Wide Fund for Nature) website provides lots of information about different habitats, including deserts.

Index